Numbers

ONE

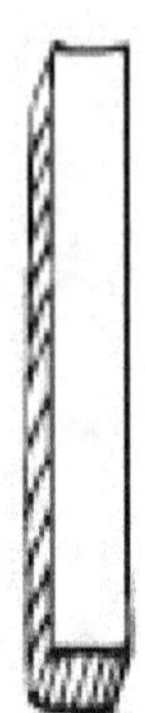

TOW

2

THREE

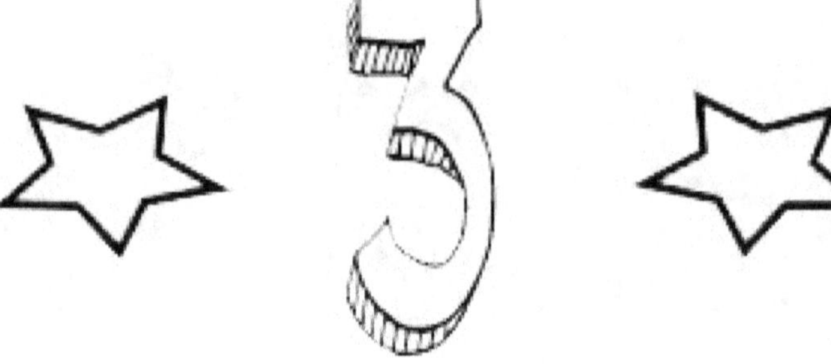

FOUR

4

FIVE

5

SIX

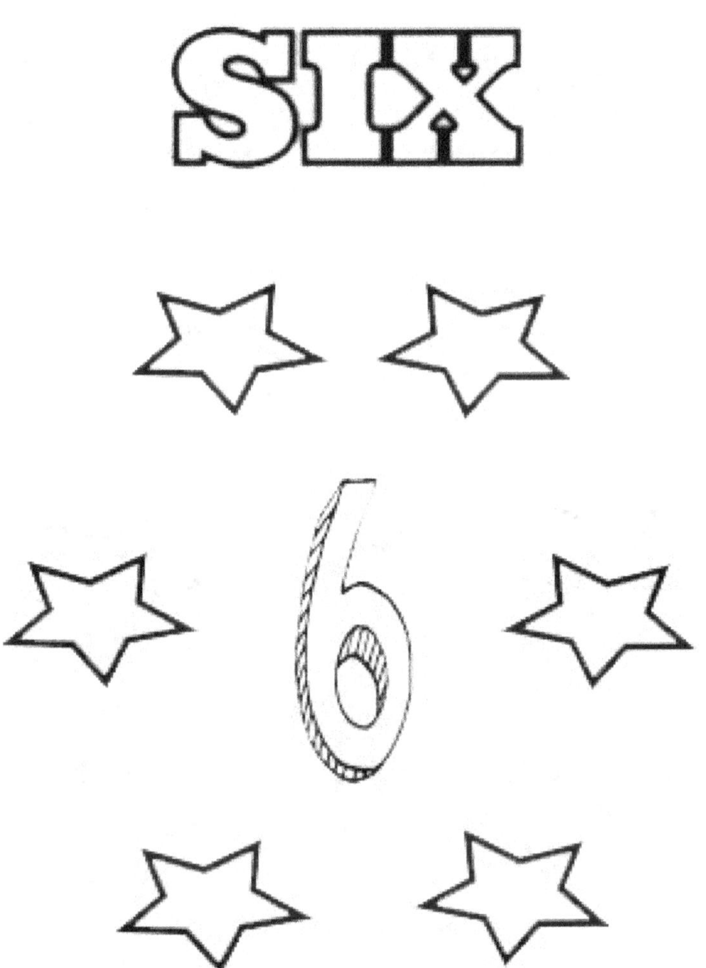

SEVEN

EIGHT

8

NINE

9

zero

Alphapets

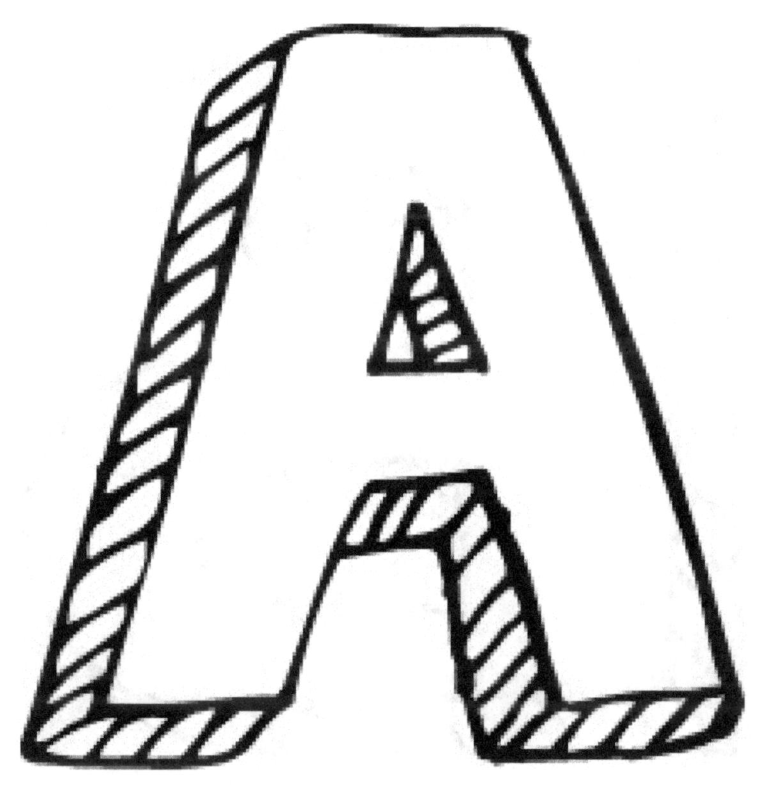

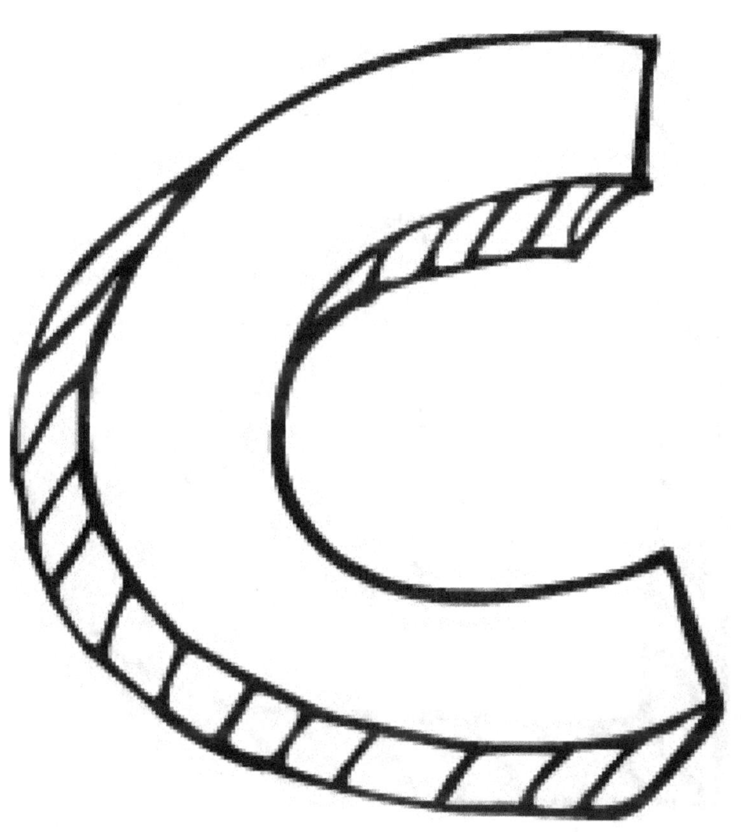

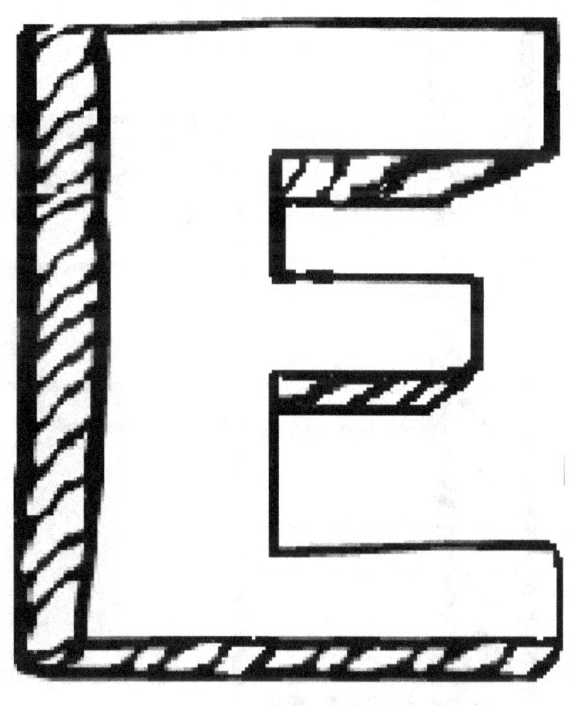

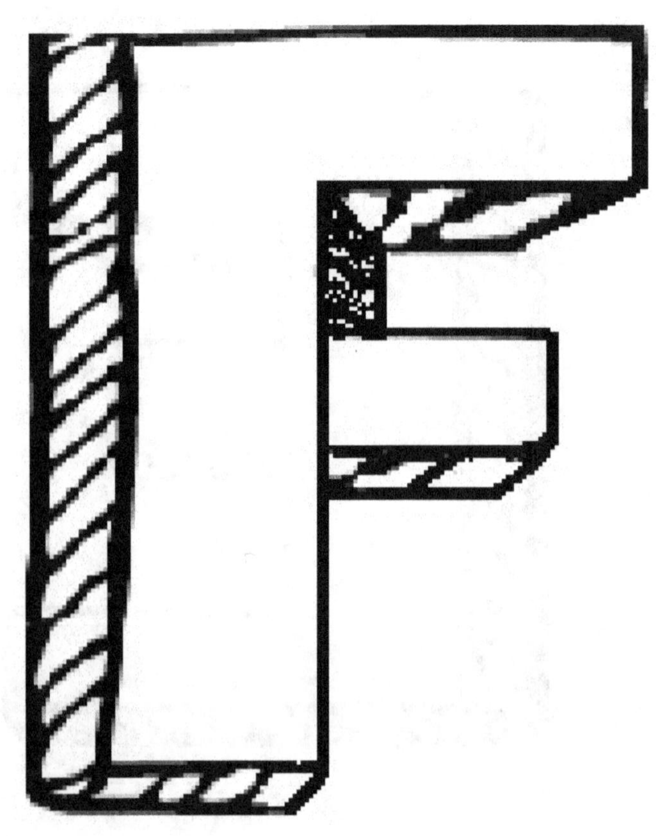

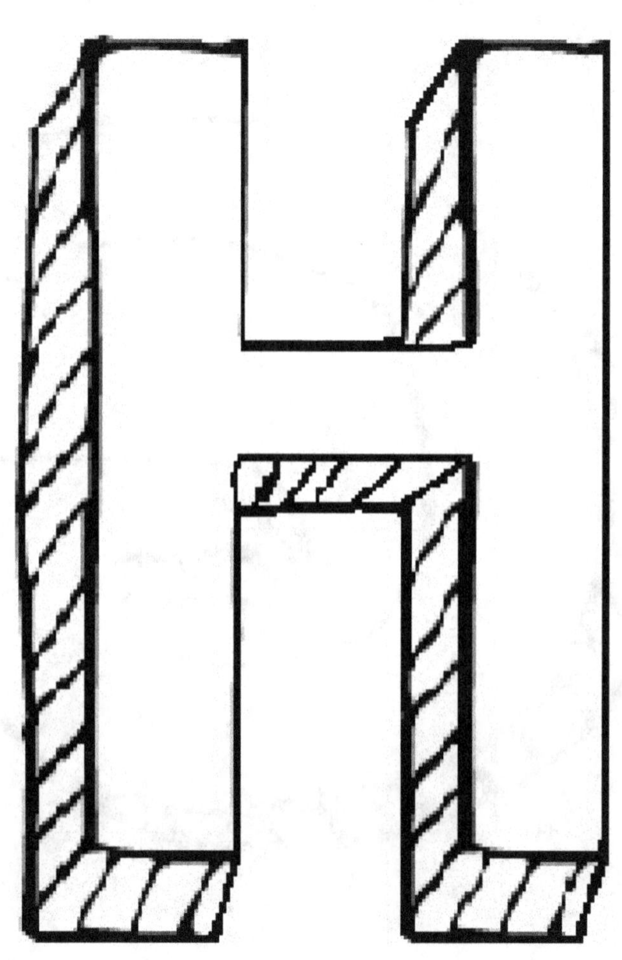

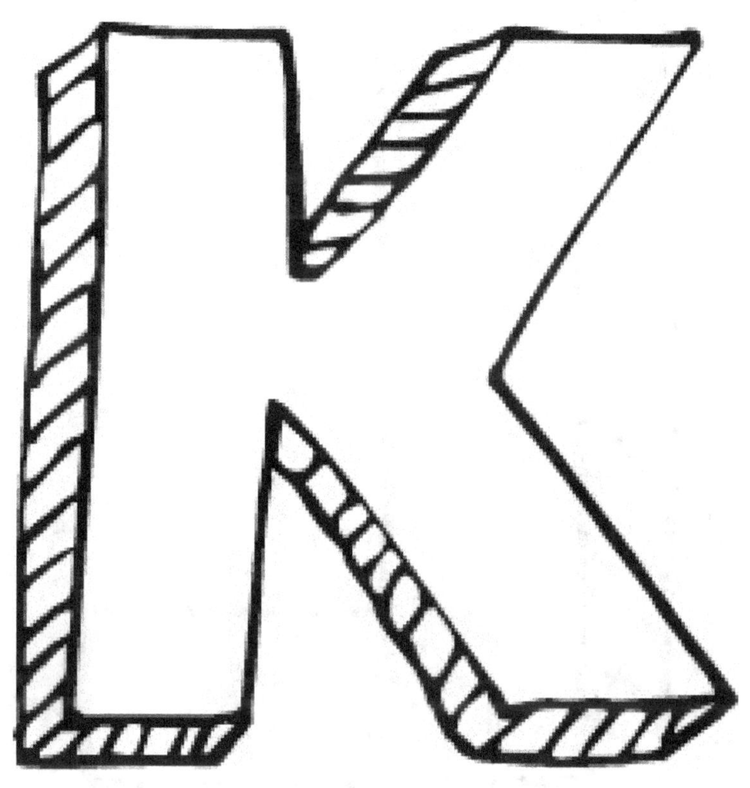

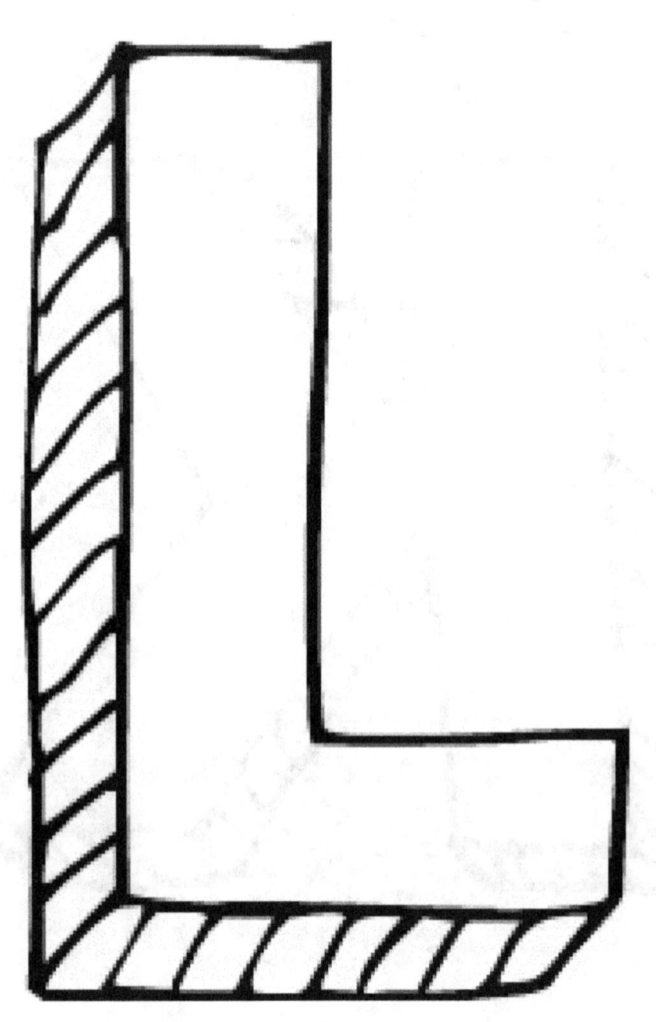

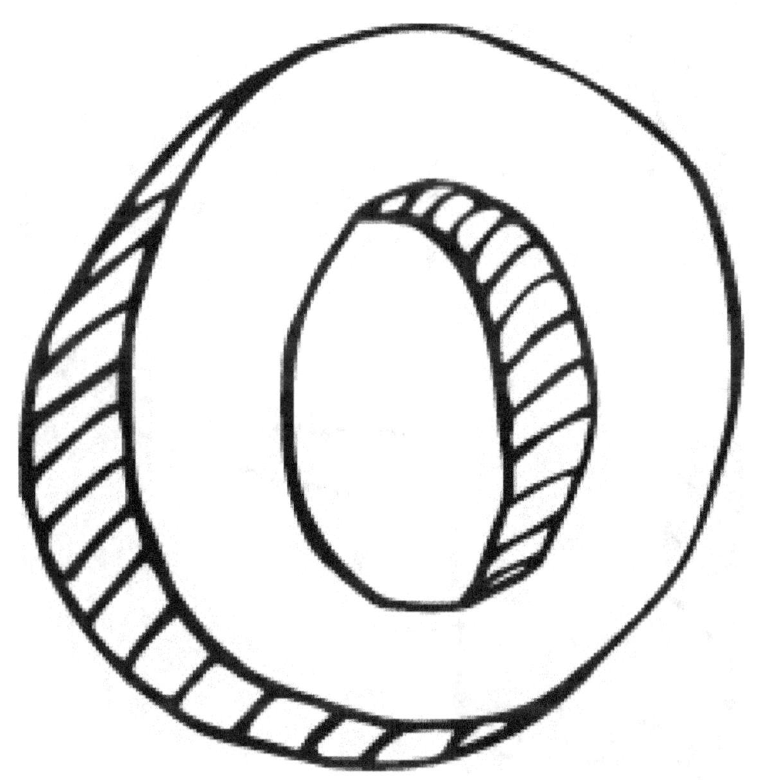

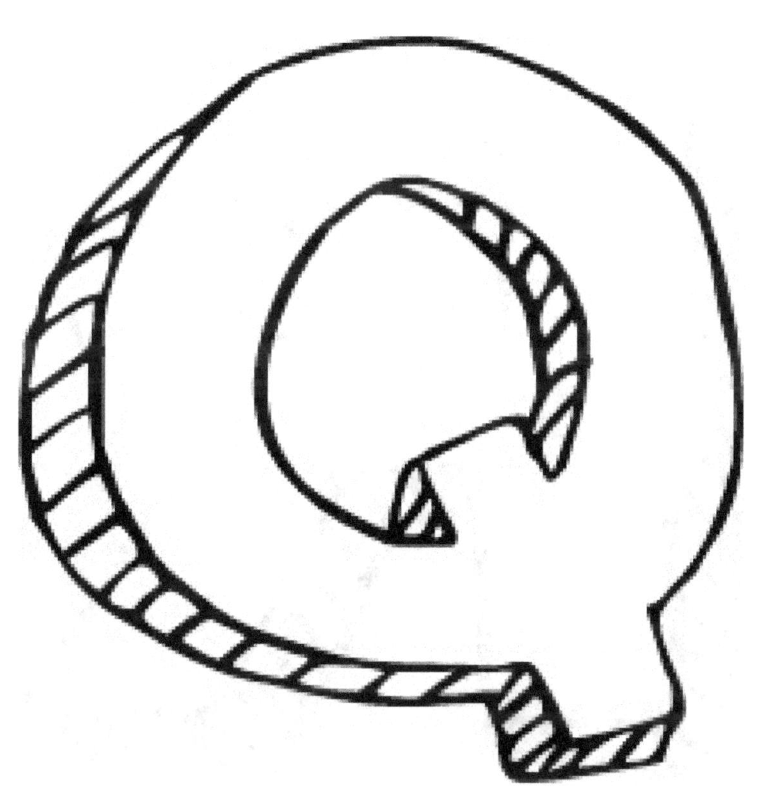

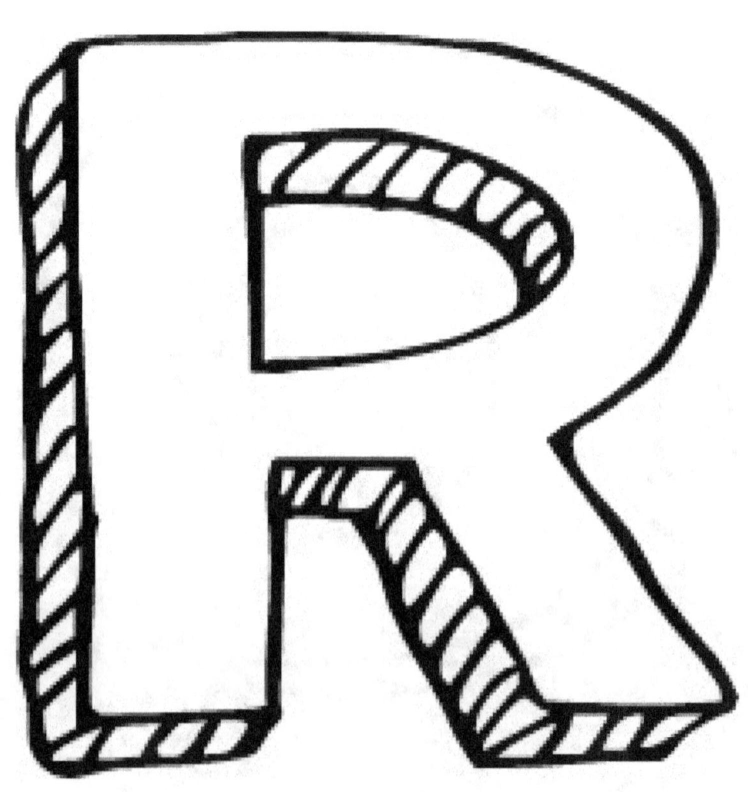

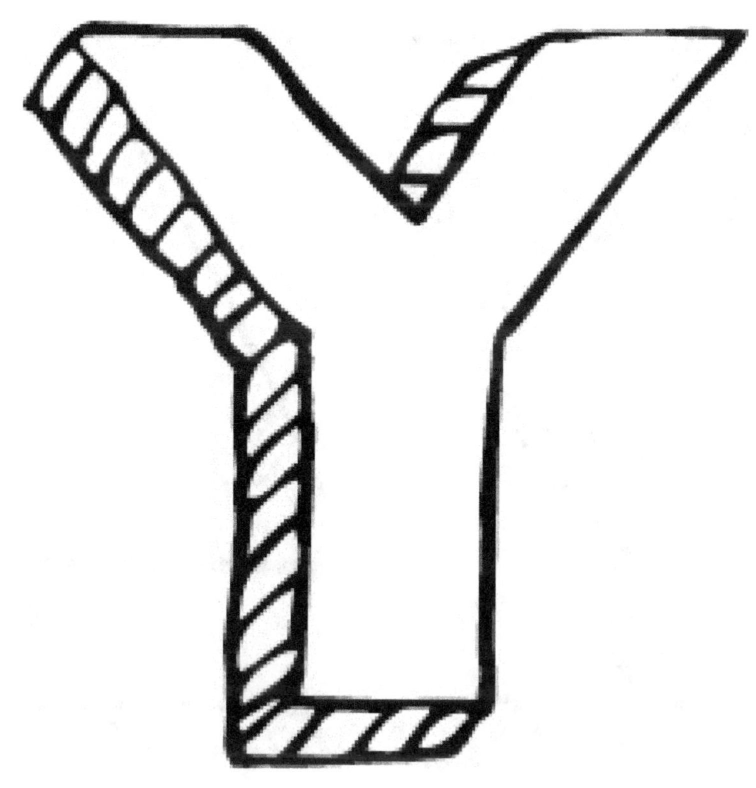

SHapes

SQUARE

RECTANGLE

CIRCLE

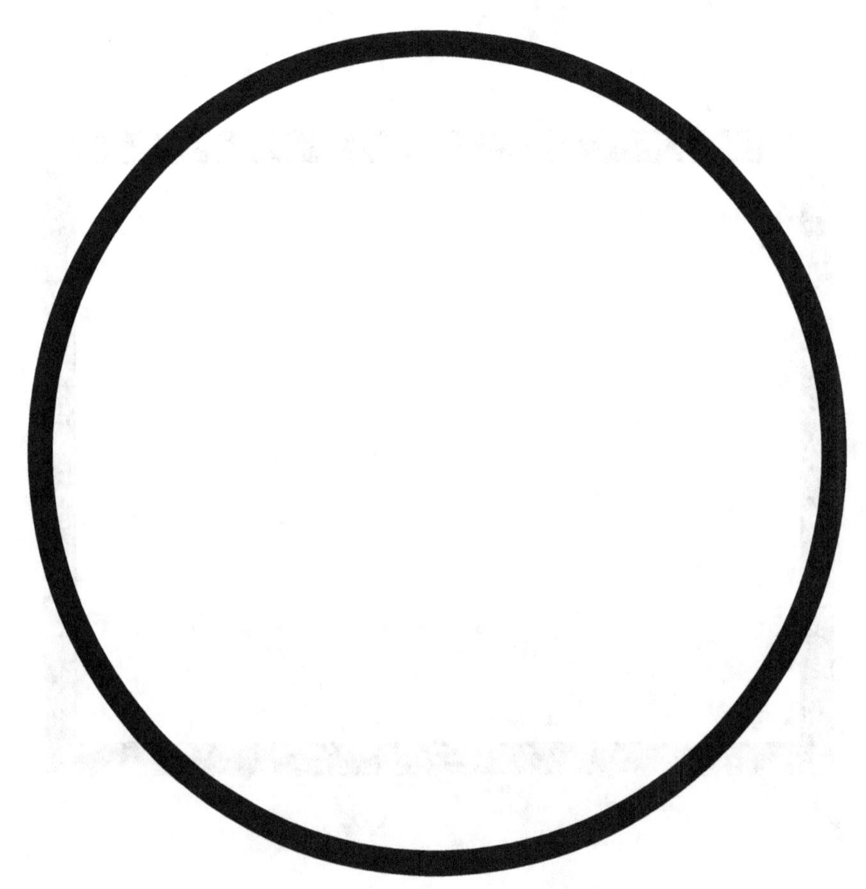

TRIANGLE

HEXAGON

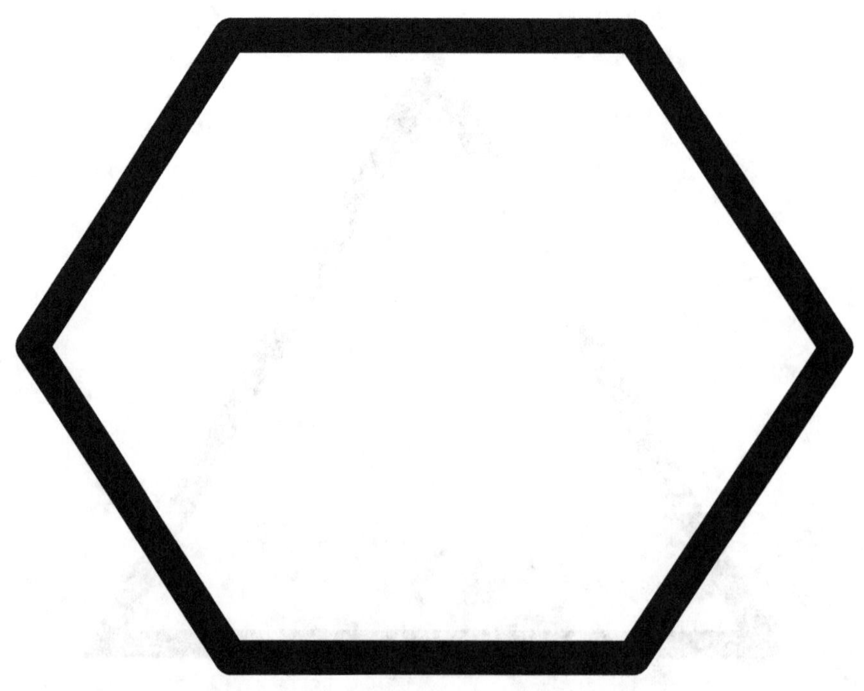

STAR

HEART

CYLINDER

CRESCENT

DAYS OF THE WEEK

Monday

Tuesday

Wednesday

Thursday

Friday

Saturday

Sunday

DOODLES

BORDER

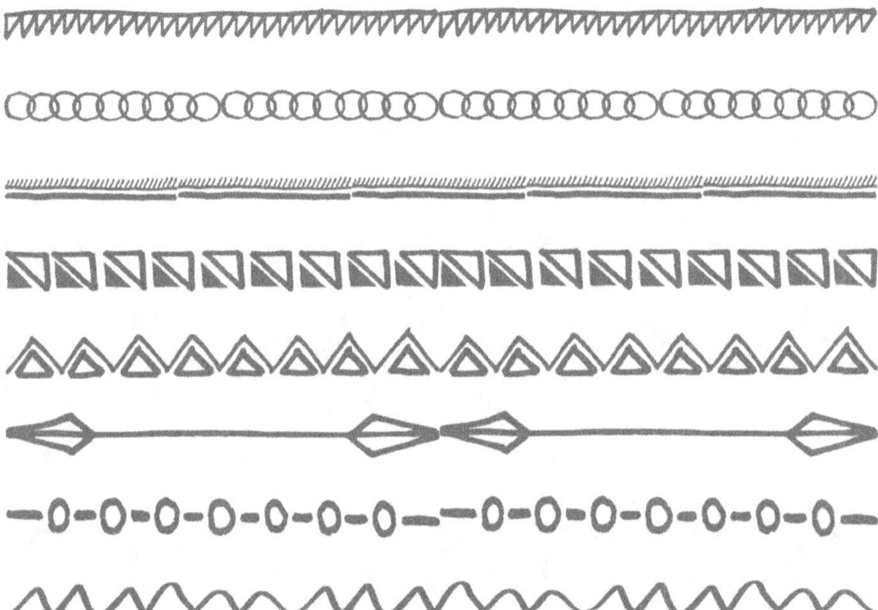

CARTOON

SHAPES

HEARTS

FLOWERS

PATTERN

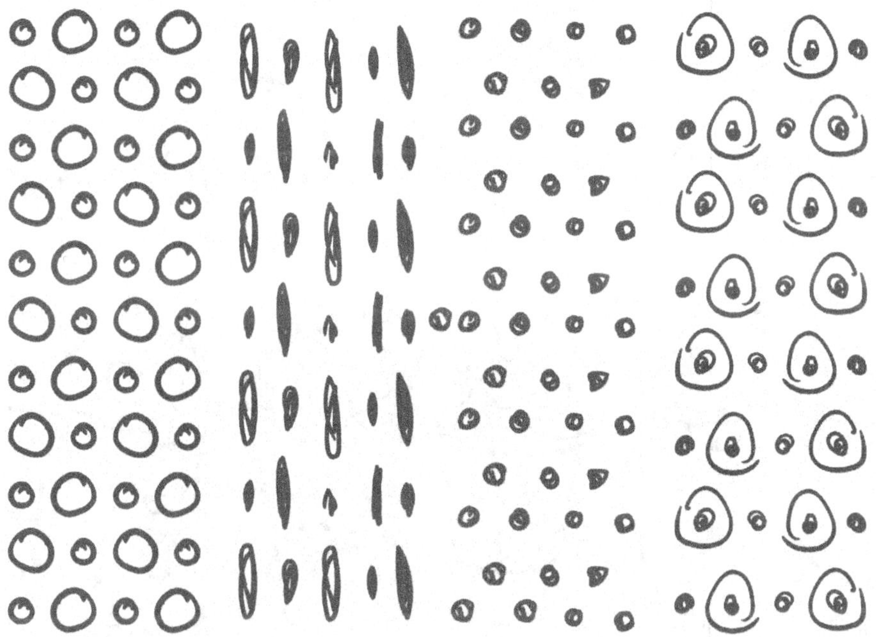

ICE

SCHOOL

BIRD

ANIMALS

OSTRICH

RHINO

COW

DEER

CAMEL

RABBIT

SHARK

SHEEP

ELEPHANT

MONKEY

KANGAROO

LION

FISH

MOUSE

CAT

DOG

GIRAFFE

DINOSAUR